10

A Brief Analysis of The

Ten

Commandments

of Almighty God

10

A Brief Analysis of The

Ten

Commandments

of Almighty God

Richard Griffin

Grace Point Publishing

This work is intended for personal edification and is the opinion of the author based on the Ten Commandments as written in the Book of Exodus, taken from the Douay Bible which was translated from the Latin Vulgate first published by the English College at Douay in 1609 and revised from 1749-1752 by Bishop Richard Challoner, edition date 11/18/1938. This edition was chosen because of the unique beauty of its prose and use of pronouns edifying Almighty God. Though believed to be accurate, aside from scripture verses in italics, the author makes no claims as to the accuracy of any information cited in this work.

Edited by

Kyle Griffin

ISBN: 978-0-9835496-4-2

Introduction

It would be reasonably accurate to state that most Christians and Jews are familiar with the Ten Commandments written in the Book of Exodus. Aside from religious education, artistic renderings are displayed in many places such as schools, courthouses and churches. The Commandments are even featured prominently on the United States Supreme Court building, rightly so, as they are the heart of law in the United States.

Just what are the Ten Commandments? They are the spoken word of I AM WHO AM, the written imperative of Almighty God in Heaven which have served as the foundation for the moral code in law for western civilization. While not the only laws handed down by God, these are the primary statutes for people to live by that were actually set into stone. The physical Ten Commandments, God's Covenant, were two stone tablets which were kept inside a special chest called the Ark of the Covenant. Gilded with gold, the Ark was also believed to hold Aaron's staff, a jar of manna, and the first Torah scroll written by Moses.

Sometimes referred to as the Decalogue, the Ten Commandments are a set of biblical laws pertaining to worship, morality and behavior. To believers, they are the beginning of wisdom and the guiding principles regarding every sin of man. Commitment to them reveals a path to understanding the will and spirit of God, and helps Christians connect with the saving grace of Jesus Christ.

When God established the Ten Commandments He arranged them with divine order. The first four instruct us as to what our relationship with Him should be and through which He establishes His Godhead. The remaining six commandments are directed at mankind's interpersonal relationships, thereby setting the foundation for proper human behavior.

As part of the compelling drama and struggle of a people trying to survive and carry out the will of God, the process of conveying the Ten Commandments to the Hebrews was a lengthy one, not accomplished in a single day. The scriptural timeline suggests it took a period of weeks for the first stone tablets to emerge, but the exact time frame is not known and can only be estimated based on what scripture reveals. We don't always know the exact length of time Moses stayed on the mount each time he went up, except for those intervals when it is specified.

We assume, for example, that when God first spoke the Ten Commandments it lasted no more than a day. The length of time it actually took for the thousands to gather at the mount before the Lord descended in smoke and thunder could have amounted to several days.

Consider the scriptural time frame forty days and forty nights. "At the time among the Jews, the number forty wasn't generally used to signify a specific number, per se, but rather more used as a general term for a large figure. When it was used in terms of time, it simply meant a "long time". Thus, the phrase "40 days and 40 nights" was just another way to say a "really long time". The number forty also had great symbolic meaning to the Jews. The number forty when used in terms of time, represents a period of probation, trial, and chastisement"[1], such as when they wandered for 40 years in the desert.

The Ten Commandments, nevertheless, are more than a rudimentary set of rules. They are a matchless unique glimpse of Almighty God. It is through the process of imparting the Ten Commandments that God manifests Himself to the Hebrews, seeking to covenant (promise, make a pact, or contract) with them through Moses by descending upon Mount Sinai in a spectacular exhibition of sight and sound, unparalleled in human history, to explain who He is, what He wants and what He requires. God gives written instructions on how to live life, interact with Him and be in His will leaving no doubt in the eyes of the Hebrews that He is the Almighty and All Powerful, the One and only God. Despite this, they would repeatedly abandon Him only to return again and again.

Hebrews, Children of Israel, Israelites, Jews

Hebrew is the early name ascribed to Jews during their days as nomads prior to the Exodus. "One explanation suggests that the term comes from a word that means "the other side," a possible reference to the fact that Abraham hailed from the other side of the Euphrates River."[2] "Another suggestion attests a relationship with the seminomadic people called Habiru who are recorded in Egyptian inscriptions."[3] True origin of the term, however, is inexact.

When Jacob, the son of Isaac, returned to Canaan the Book of Genesis says he wrestled with an angel who gave him the name Israel, hence all his descendants became known as the 'Children of Israel.'

"The term Jew comes from the word Yehudi, a description for members of the tribe of Judah, which developed after the death of King Solomon when a rift occurred between the tribes of Israel and the tribe of Judah. When the two groups reunited they formed the kingdom of Israel (Israelite) whose religion is called Judaism."[4] The terms are sometimes used synonymously today when referring to the Jewish people.

Moses

Approximately 1526 B.C., after the death of Joseph who was believed to be second in command to Pharaoh "Ahmose I"[6] and the youngest son of Jacob the patriarch, a new ruler ascended the throne in Egypt, "Amenhotep I".[6] This new Pharaoh worried that the Children of Israel would either overpower them, or join together with a foreign force and leave Egypt. This would foreseeably have a huge economic impact on the country because the Hebrews were a large segment of the workforce. They also outnumbered the Egyptians. So Amenhotep enslaved them and decreed that all newborn male Hebrew children be killed in an effort to control their population. During this terror one boy born of the tribe of Levi was concealed by his mother who after three months could no longer hide him. Placing him in a basket among the reeds on the bank of the Nile, he was discovered by Pharaoh's daughter. "In the Biblical account, the daughter of Pharaoh who rescued Moses is not named. A daughter of Pharaoh named Bithiah is mentioned in I Chronicles 4:18. The Midrash (Jewish tradition) identifies the two as the same person, and says she received her name, literally "daughter of Yah", Yah being a form of YHWH, which is often rendered in English as "LORD", because of her compassion and pity in saving the infant Moses. It relates Leviticus Rabbah 1:3(Jewish Tradition) how God said He will take her in and call her YHWH's daughter, which is what "Bithiah" means, because she took in a child not her own, and called him her son (Moses can mean "child" in Egyptian."[5] In a twist of irony, Moses' own mother was hired by Pharaoh's daughter to care for him. When "Amenhotep died in 1506 BC"[6] Moses could have become the next Pharaoh of Egypt.

As a grown man, knowing he too was a child of Israel from his own circumcision, Moses must have felt a connection to his people and their plight causing him to secretly slay an Egyptian guard for beating a fellow Hebrew. The act was discovered forcing him to flee Egypt, as the current king, possibly "Thutmose II"[7] sought to kill him for what he had done. He found refuge in the land of Midian where he bested shepherds who had harried the daughters of Jethro at a well while they were watering their flocks. Having ingratiated himself to Jethro, Moses was given one of his daughters to marry. He served Jethro as a shepherd, and one day while leading the flocks, Moses approached Mount Sinai and had his first encounter with God who called to him from a 'burning bush.' God disclosed that He had heard the cry of the Hebrews in bondage and was sending Moses to lead them out of Egypt so they could come worship Him at this holy mountain.

God said to him; *For I will stretch forth My hand and will strike Egypt with all My wonders which I will do in the midst of them: after these he will let you go. And I will give favor to this people, in the sight of the Egyptians: and when you go forth, you shall not depart empty: But every woman shall ask of her neighbor, and of her that is in her house, vessels of silver and of gold, and raiment: and you shall put them on your sons and daughters, and shall spoil Egypt.* Ex. III vs. 20 – 22.

Throughout history people are born to be specifically called by God for select purposes. Some for a singular function, such as Judas Iscariot, the betrayer of Jesus, while others for great tasks, like Noah, to build the Ark. Moses was one such person. His destiny began at birth, saved by the daughter of the very king who condemned him to death, who then raised him as an Egyptian prince.

Moses was likely a strong individual, well trained in warfare as a prince of Egypt would be. This probably accounted for his ability to kill the Egyptian guard and best the shepherds at the well of Jethro. He was impressive enough that Jethro took him into his family and gave him his daughter, Zipporah, to be his wife. Had he not been called by God, Moses may have been quite content to remain a shepherd, but God's purpose for him had not yet been fulfilled, a purpose which would take his entire life to complete. He would return to Egypt, confront Pharaoh, lead his people through the Red Sea and receive the Ten Laws from God Himself atop Mount Sinai.

Mount Sinai

God's holy mountain, Mount Sinai, also called the Mountain of Moses, Mount Horeb, Har Sinai and Jabal Musa, is located in the southern end of Egypt's Sinai Peninsula between the Gulf of Suez and the Gulf of Aqaba. The peninsula is a triangular desert of arid lands and rocky mountainous terrain. Moderately crowded by slightly taller peaks, "i.e. Mount Catherine, 8,625 feet, Mount Sinai rises 7,497 feet above sea level."[8]

Though not singularly spectacular, it is a barren granite massif rising from red sandy plains having a distinguishing promontory with a crescent shaped amphitheater near the top where the 70 Hebrew elders, called ancients, waited for Moses while he spoke with God in the cloud. "There is also a cave at the summit named the Moses Cave because it is believed to be where Moses waited to receive the tablets on which the Ten Commandments were inscribed.

Today, visitors to Mount Sinai can climb to the summit via the Path of Moses, a stairway of nearly 4,000 steps."9

Though debated, Mount Sinai's current location is generally accepted to be the same as the biblical Mount Sinai. Scripture would seem to support the present site, as it states that while Moses was in Midian, located east of the peninsula, he led his flocks west into the wilderness when he came upon the burning bush.

Scripture also tells of the Hebrews setting out from a resting place called "Rephidim in the Wadi Feiran, (wadi; Arabic for a valley, or ravine that is dry except during the rainy season) near its junction with the Wadi esh-Sheikh"10 which is just to the west of Mount Sinai. These two references would place Mount Sinai in Egypt, within the Sinai Peninsula, in variance to Saudi Arabia, as some have suggested.

The Scriptural Narrative

Three months and 300 miles after fleeing through the Red Sea from Pharaoh, possibly "Thutmoses III"11 not Ramesses II, as has been popularly portrayed in the movies, Moses and the Hebrews arrived at the base of God's holy mountain. Shortly after their camp was established Moses went up to the summit where God called to him. God expressed His desire to make a covenant with this chosen people and establish a special relationship with them separate from other peoples of the Earth who worshipped only false gods. The Lord asked Moses to inform the people;

You have seen what I have done to the Egyptians, how I have carried you upon the wings of eagles, and have taken you to Myself. If therefore you will hear My voice, and keep My covenant, you shall be My peculiar possession above all people: for all the earth is Mine. Ex. 19 vs. 4 – 5.

Moses delivered God's message. Returning to the Lord he advised that the people would do all that the Lord has spoken. Once an agreement had been established, God told Moses He would appear to the people in three days, even describing how He would come into view, admonishing him to set a boundary at the base of the mountain, warning them that they should not venture beyond the limit set by Moses.

Lo, now will I come to thee in the darkness of a cloud, that the people may hear Me speaking to thee, and may believe thee forever. And Moses told the words of the people to the Lord. And He said to him: Go to the people, and sanctify them today, and tomorrow, and let them wash their garments. And let them be ready against the third day: for on the third day the Lord will come down in the sight of all the people upon Mount Sinai. And thou shalt appoint certain limits to the people round about, and thou shalt say to them: Take heed you go not up into the mount, and that ye touch not the borders thereof: every one that toucheth the mount dying he shall die. Ex. 19 vs. 9 – 12.

The agreement to covenant with God launched the process which would culminate in Moses carrying two sets of stone tablets down the mountain to the Hebrews. It is important to note here that every time Moses ascended the mount he had to climb a mile and a half to reach the summit, a rocky hike of which takes approximately 3 hours today up modern steps. So, in real terms, it conceivably took Moses at least one full day to meet with God and report back to the people about what the Lord had spoken.

On the third day, as Moses had foretold, God descended upon Mount Sinai exactly as He had said, in a dark cloud and not without special effects. Even today, such a display would be a wondrous and intimidating event to behold. One can only imagine the barrage on the senses witnessing God Almighty come down to Earth, in smoke, fire, lightning, thunder, trumpet blaring and ground shaking.

And now the third day was come, and the morning appeared: and behold, thunders began to be heard and lightning to flash and the noise of a trumpet sounded exceeding loud: and the people that was in the camp feared. And when Moses had brought them forth to meet God from the place of the camp, they stood at the bottom of the mount. And all Mount Sinai was on a smoke: because the Lord was come down upon it in fire, and the smoke arose from it as out of a furnace: and all the mount was terrible. And the sound of the trumpet grew by degrees louder and louder, and was drawn out to a greater length:
Moses spoke, and God answered him. Ex. 19 vs. 16 – 19.

We don't know how long this display went on, but after some length of time God called Moses up to the mount again, charging him a second time not to allow the people to come up lest they die. Obedient to God, Moses returned to the people and when he had finished cautioning them not to cross the boundary, they heard the Lord's voice. *And the Lord spoke all these words;* Ex. 20 vs. 1.

The words they heard were those of the Ten Commandments. But did God actually speak to the people, or was he speaking in a voice that was unintelligible to everyone except Moses, who reiterated God's word? Consider the following verses taken in chronological order.

Lo, now will I come to thee in the darkness of a cloud, that the people may hear me speaking to thee, and may believe thee forever. Ex. 19 vs. 9.

Having agreed to a covenant with the people, the Lord instructed Moses to tell the people to prepare for a visit from Him, in three days, at which time He would speak to them that they might believe in Him.

It is now the third day and the people are prepared and waiting at the base of Mount Sinai for the Lord to arrive. They are careful to heed the boundary limit set by God when they observe a dark cloud descend upon the mountain with thunder, lightning and the sound of a trumpet. The Lord had arrived, and his first words to the Hebrews were those of the Ten Commandments.

When God had finished speaking the words of the Ten Commandments scripture tells us that the Hebrews were so afraid that they moved away from the base of Mount Sinai imploring Moses to speak on God's behalf. One can only imagine what it must have been like that day. Being in God's presence and hearing Him speak was just too terrifying. So out of fear of death and the power of God they asked Moses to speak for Him.

And all the people saw the voices and the flames, and the sound of the trumpet, and the mount smoking: and being terrified and struck with fear, they stood afar off, saying to Moses: Speak thou to us, and we will hear: let not the Lord speak to us, lest we die. Ex. 20 vs. 18 – 19.

Happily for the Hebrews, God agreed. In the wake of the Ten Commandments God outlined a substantial list of judgments, punishments and laws which served to elaborate upon the Lord's instructions. For example;

He that striketh a man with a will to kill him shall be put to death. Ex. 21 vs. 12.

If a thief be found breaking open a house or undermining it, and be wounded so as to die: he that slew him shall not be guilty of blood. Ex. 22 vs. 12

Thou shalt not follow the multitude to do evil; Ex. 23 vs. 2.

Neither shalt thou take bribes, which even blind the wise, and pervert the words of the just. Ex. 23 vs. 8.

When the Lord had finished pronouncing His judgments He ordered Moses to return to the camp and reveal to the people all that was written down in the book. The Hebrews must have been anxiously awaiting God's word for when Moses had finished reading the additional terms they responded with one voice.

We will do all the words of the Lord, which He hath spoken. Ex. 24 vs. 3.

Having read the judgments of God, and having ratified His covenant, Moses built an altar at the foot of the mount the following morning and the twelve tribes of Israel offered holocausts, and sacrificed victims of calves to the Lord. Moses wrote down all the words of the Lord in the Book of the Covenant called Elle Haddebarim by the Hebrews, better known today as the Book of Deuteronomy. In it Moses reminded God's newly chosen people of all that they had seen and heard;

And you came to the foot of the mount, which burned even unto heaven: and there was darkness, and a cloud and obscurity in it. And the Lord spoke to you from the midst of the fire. You heard the voice of his words, but you saw not any form at all. Deut. 4 vs. 12.

Now when the sacrifices and celebration had ended Moses brought Aaron, Nadab, Abiu, and seventy of the ancients up to the mount where scripture says they saw God. There is even a partial reference of what they witnessed;

And under his feet, as it were, a work of sapphire stone, and as the heaven, when clear. Ex. 24 vs. 10.

It is impossible to know precisely what manifestation of God the elders were being permitted to see because not even Moses was ever allowed to gaze upon God's face. However, we can reasonably assume that what they did see was recognized as being somewhat like themselves, based partly on how God was hereby described, and by what other scriptural references tell us.

Whosoever shall shed man's blood, his blood shall be shed: for man was made to the image of God. Gen. 9 vs. 6.

God created man of the earth, and made him after his own image. Ecclesiasticus 17 vs. 1.

In whom the god of this world hath blinded the minds of unbelievers, that the light of the gospel of the glory of Christ, who is the image of God. 2 Cor. 4 vs. 4.

By it we bless God and the Father: and by it we curse men, who are made after the likeness of God. James 3 vs. 9.

Some would argue that we are not really made to look like God for He is spirit; therefore the resemblance to God regards the soul, not the body. And yet scripture speaks of God as Father, and Jesus as Son of the Father, and clearly we are made to resemble God, and if so, how? Admittedly, God is spirit and not flesh, but does that have to mean that His spirit is formless, or having no shape? Or would it make more sense for God's spirit to have a divine form that is mirrored in his creation of man? And isn't Jesus Christ the image of God made flesh? And when angels appear to the sons of men, do they not look as men?

And God said: Let us make man to our image and likeness: and let him have dominion over the fishes of the sea, and the fowls of the air, and the beasts, and the whole earth, and every creeping creature that moveth upon the earth. And God created man to his own image: to the image of God he created him: male and female he created them. Let us make man to our image and likeness. Gen. 1 vs. 26 – 27

Having ascended Mount Sinai they arrived at a place where they had an opportunity to view God, yet not be directly in God's presence. That was reserved for Moses alone.

And the Lord said to Moses: Come up to me into the mount, and be there: and I will give thee tables of stone, and the law, and the commandments which I have written: that thou mayst teach them. Ex. 24 vs. 12.

Moses waited on the Lord for six days and on the seventh day God called to him from within the cloud.

And the sight of the glory of the Lord was like a burning fire upon the top of the mount, in the eyes of the children of Israel. And Moses entering into the midst of the cloud went up into the mountain and was there forty days and forty nights. Ex. 24 vs. 17 – 18.

The stone tablets on which the Ten Commandments were recorded and written in God's own hand were of such significance to God, that over the next forty days He outlined to Moses how to construct the Ark of the Covenant in which they were to be placed, along with the tabernacle that would house them and provide a place for the Lord to sit and show His mercy. God had a precisely defined pattern with which he charged Moses regarding the design, materials, construction methods, measurements, items, clothing and furniture, along with their explicit uses and placement, right down to the candle snuffers and an altar to burn incense, an act described as "an emblem of prayer, ascending to God from an inflamed heart."[12] And when God had finished giving all his instructions He presented Moses with the two stone tablets.

And the Lord, when he had ended these words in Mount Sinai, gave to Moses two stone tables of testimony, written with the finger of God. Ex. 31 vs. 18

Two events transpired over the forty days Moses was with the Lord on Mount Sinai. The first, just described, occurred between Moses and God. The second involved Aaron and the Hebrews in the camp at the foot of the mountain. They had been waiting for Moses to return. His delay resulted in a lack of religious direction, and uncertainty regarding Moses. Their impatience caused them to revert to traditional gods they had come to know while in captivity. Since bull worship was common in Egypt some of the Hebrews demanded that they continue to worship a god, the golden calf, which was familiar to them, instead of the Lord God with whom they were being reacquainted. Why Aaron, who knew the power of God as well as Moses, opted to form a calf of gold for this group is not that mysterious. "First of all, he was Moses' alternate while Moses was on the mount. The people would naturally approach him with important issues. He was not, however, a leader, and he was obviously weaker than Moses in spite of all that he had seen. Secondly, he possessed the necessary metal working skills required to melt the gold earrings taken from the people with which to form the idol of the calf. Third, he may have been afraid of this unmanageable group, and although sinful, he was attempting to combine the powerful God who had delivered them with the pagan worship they were accustomed to in Egypt."[13]

The Lord God was aware of what had been happening in the camp. His anger had been kindled against the Hebrews because of this and he wanted to destroy them making a new people out of Moses.

And the Lord spoke to Moses, saying: Go, get thee down: thy people, which thou hast brought out of the land of Egypt, hath sinned. They have quickly strayed from the way which thou didst shew them: and they have made to themselves a molten calf, and have adored it, and sacrificing victims to it, have said: These are thy gods, O Israel, that have brought thee out of the land of Egypt. And again the Lord said to Moses: See that this people is stiff necked: Let me alone, that my wrath may be kindled against them, and that I may destroy them, and I will make of thee a great nation. Ex. 32 vs. 7 – 10.

But Moses did not want to waste all that the Lord had accomplished through him just to start all over again. He recognized that the Hebrews already had a good start on the population and hoped to salvage that. Moses also worried about how the Egyptians would perceive God who had rescued His people then proceeded to extinguish them. So, he pleaded with the Lord not to destroy the multitude, and the Lord acquiesced.

When Moses returned with the two stone tablets and observed what God had foretold about what had transpired in the camp, he became angry and threw them down breaking them into pieces. Moses destroyed the golden calf and then gave the people a choice; join him on the side of the Lord, or not, which the sons of Levi did, meaning all men, women and children who were descended from the tribe of Levi. Moses then commanded that everyone else be destroyed.

Then standing in the gate of the camp, he said: If any man be on the Lord's side let him join with me. And all the sons of Levi gathered themselves together unto him: And he said to them: Thus saith the Lord God of Israel: Put every man his sword upon his thigh: go, and return from gate to gate through the midst of the camp, and let every man kill his brother, and friend, and neighbor. And the sons of Levi did according to the words of Moses, and there were slain that day about three and twenty thousand men. Ex. 32 vs. 26 – 28.

It wasn't until after the tabernacle had been constructed that God spoke to Moses regarding the second set of tablets. This period between the first and second sets was undoubtedly quite long, perhaps several months, considering the logistics and time it must have taken to manufacture the numerous items God required, for they had not yet been made. When the tabernacle was completed Moses met with God and was instructed, as before, to make two new tablets on which the Lord would once again write the ten laws. Forty days and nights later Moses appeared with the new tablets and his face glowed with the glory of God.

And after this he said: Hew thee two tables of stone like unto the former, and I will write upon them the words which were in the tables, which thou brokest. Be ready in the morning, that thou mayst forthwith go up into Mount Sinai, and thou shalt stand with me upon the top of the mount. Let no man go up with thee: and let not any man be seen throughout all the mount: neither let the oxen nor the sheep feed over against it. Then he cut out two tables of stone, such as had been before: and rising very early he went up into Mount Sinai, as the Lord had commanded him, carrying with him the tables. And when the Lord was come down in a cloud,

Moses stood with him, calling upon the name of the Lord. And the Lord said to Moses: Write these words by which I have made a covenant both with thee and with Israel. Ex. 34 vs. 1 – 5.

And he was there with the Lord forty days and forty nights: he neither ate bread nor drank water, and He wrote upon the tables the ten words of the covenant. And when Moses came down from Mount Sinai, he held the two tables of the testimony, and he knew not that his face was horned from the conversation of the Lord. Ex. 34 vs. 28 – 29.

A note regarding this last verse; "Moses has been depicted in medieval art as having horns on his head, similar to animals, as in Michelangelo's sculpture, Moses. This was based on St. Jerome's misinterpretation of the Hebrew Masoretic text that uses the term karan, which often literally meant horn. The term is now understood to mean 'emitting rays', protruding as a horn. The phrase, he knew not that his face was horned, was actually meant to describe Moses' face as shining as with rays of light. St. Jerome's intention was to express Moses' face as having become glorified by his use of the Latin word for horned."[14]

There are those who would argue that the two sets of stone tablets were not the same, partly because God's conversations with Moses each time did not contain identical elements. This becomes obvious when comparing the scriptural text regarding the two events. There is also the fact that God addressed the people with the first set of tablets, but spoke only to Moses regarding the second set. This has no effect on the Ten Commandments themselves because the second set was identical to the first.

God said to Moses: *Hew thee two tables of stone like unto the former, and I will write upon them the words which were in the tables, which thou brokest.* Ex. 34 vs. 1

THE TEN COMMANDMENTS

And the Lord spoke all these words:

ONE

I am the Lord thy God,

who brought thee out of the land of Egypt,

out of the house of bondage.

Thou shalt not have strange gods before Me.

The Hebrews spent 400 years in Egypt which had been foretold by God to Abram prior to their exodus;

A deep sleep fell upon Abram and a great and darksome horror seized upon him. And it was said unto him; Know thou beforehand that thy seed shall be a stranger in a land not their own, and they shall bring them under bondage, and afflict them four hundred years. But I will judge the nation which they shall serve, and after this they shall come out with great substance. Gen. 15 vs. 13 – 14.

During that time the Hebrews were exposed to a wide range of false gods that proliferated Egypt and Asia. They worshiped and crafted idols to many of them and often embraced several gods at once. After leaving Egypt the Children of Israel would interact with other nations and encounter other gods. Deities such as Moloch had children and young virgins sacrificed to them as a means of ensuring the safety of a society, or to get them through times of famine. During certain periods all first male children were required to be sacrificed. Ashteroth (Astarte/Ishtar) was the goddess of fertility, sexuality and war. Sexual promiscuity was a significant ritual for this deity. Baal could refer to any number of gods that were worshiped for almost any reason including weather and agriculture, or as patrons of the city. Belial is also mentioned in scripture, though the reference is not as a deity per se, but rather a derogatory phrase, or description. The sons of Eli were called sons of Belial meaning they were 'worthless men'. It also referred to those who turned away from God and committed sacrilege in the sanctuary. Belial is also a reference to Satan.

God obviously wanted no competition from any mere worldly deity and demanded this first and foremost, by reminding the Hebrews He was the one who led them from bondage through a series of formidable demonstrations of His power and might, which no other gods possessed.

Today there are five major religions in the world today; Judaism, Christianity, Hinduism, Buddhism and Islam. Judaism is the distinct religion of the Jewish people. Christians and Jews believe in the same Almighty God, however, Christians recognize Jesus Christ as the Son of God through whom salvation is promised. Christianity is the only religion where the Son of Almighty God having been conceived of the Holy Spirit, was born, crucified raised from the dead and ascended into Heaven, all of which was witnessed by many. Early Jews struggled with many gods before accepting the one true God. Over time western man through education and enlightenment cast off pagan religions and recognize only one true God. As such, most modern Christians and Jews have little difficulty today rejecting all other religions as false.

TWO

Thou shalt not make to thyself a graven thing,
nor the likeness of anything that is in heaven above, or in the earth beneath,
nor of those things that are in the waters under the earth.
Thou shalt not adore them, nor serve them:
I am the Lord thy God,
mighty, jealous, visiting the iniquity of the fathers upon the children,
unto the third and fourth generation of them that hate me: and shewing mercy unto
thousands to them that love me, and keep my commandments.

There were many types of deities to which the nations of the world shaped images. Reminding them of his power and possessiveness, God wanted his chosen people to understand that He was the only God of Heaven and Earth and of everything that was in them. There was no room for superstitions, or any god other than the Lord. He is sufficient for all things and all purposes and He will not tolerate attention to them for any reason to the point of outlining both punishment and reward relating to this commandment. God also wanted to have fellowship through worship and adoration. Veneration to idols interferes with that and devalues mans' relationship with Him.

Today it could be argued that perhaps the worship of statues and objects, reminiscent of idols in ancient times, has been exchanged by other things like footballs, baseballs, cars, TV, cell phones and computers. We may not bow down to objects any longer, but anything that is placed above God could be considered idol worship, for example; not going to church on Sunday because it interferes with some other activity like watching the game, playing golf, or going boating. If devotion to school, making money, a career, or empty pleasure seeking displaces activities, or time normally reserved for God, those ambitions and distractions that disconnect us from God might need to be modified. Possessions, relationships, entertainment, hobbies and all sorts of addiction are modern idols, if they separate us from God.

THREE

Thou shalt not take the name of the Lord thy God in vain:
for the Lord will not hold him guiltless
that shall take the name of the Lord his God in vain.

The early Hebrews wrote God's name YHWH. It was a written representation only, having no associated pronunciation, as His name was not spoken. When Moses inquired at the burning bush the Lord revealed His name conveying His essence and nature and stating that He is eternal. But Moses was not just asking "What should I call you?" He was asking "Who are you?" acknowledging that the being whose voice emanated from the bush had immeasurable power. The Lord's response? I AM WHO AM.

God doesn't prohibit the use of His name except when it serves no honorable purpose. He is telling us not refer to Him in an irreverent, blasphemous manner, or to promote self-expression, or worthless, fruitless communication. To use His name other than in prayer, song, adoration, or educational, illustrative, or meaningful discussion is profane to say the least, and to do so will come with a consequence.

Generally speaking, people do not say "I AM WHO AM", or YHWH (today vocalized yah-wey) when referring to God. He is most often called by who and what He is, Lord and God. And in the Trinity, God is recognized as God the Father, God the Son (Jesus Christ, or Yeshua) and God the Holy Ghost, or Holy Spirit. Yet man in his love, adoration and respect has bestowed God with many other names. And though those names were not known when the Ten Commandments were written, they are still the names of God to which this commandment applies. Why? Because the names of God are more than just title, or identification. The concepts embodied in God's names reflect His nature and attributes, the totality of His being, especially

His glory. They are worthy and deserving of ultimate respect and reverence. Therefore, to say, write, or use phrases such as, Oh my God! OMG! Jesus Christ! God damn it! Sweet Jesus! Swear to God!, or any other reference to God, or the Trinity, as common everyday expletives is taking the Lord's name in vain.

FOUR

Remember that thou keep holy the Sabbath day.

Six days shalt thou labor, and shalt do all thy works.

But on the seventh day is the Sabbath of the Lord thy God:

thou shalt do no work on it,

thou nor thy son, nor thy daughter, nor thy manservant, nor thy maidservant,

nor thy beast, nor the stranger that is within thy gates.

For in six days the Lord made heaven and earth,

and the sea, and all things that are in them, and rested on the seventh day:

therefore the Lord blessed the seventh day, and sanctified it.

By establishing one day of the week as the Sabbath, or seventh day, Sunday in the Christian tradition, God was mirroring the cycle of His creation. It would be an easy reminder that every seventh day would not only be a day of rest, promoting well-being to the body, but a day of worship which God set aside for Himself. This seven day cycle is a life cycle that is in balance with the natural order of man, the world and creation. Just as there is a balance between night and day, sleep and wakefulness, periods of hunger, birth and death, husband and wife, moreover, there is a balance of work and worship to God. He tells us that the seventh day is sanctified, blessed and His special day for us to keep holy.

The most basic meaning of the word holy is to be "set apart", or "dedicated" to God. Being dedicated to God requires a conscious recognition of its importance. We can accomplish this by reading God's word, prayer and by attending church. Church offers us the opportunity to fellowship with other believers, sing earnest praise, listen to teaching, pray, hear the Word of God and show obedience, reverence and devotion to the Lord. It is a public affirmation of faith and dedication to Him. But that doesn't let us off the hook for the rest of the day. Regardless of where, or how we spend this holy day, we should be contemplating God's command to keep the day holy all day long. He should be our first thought through every activity this day and every day.

FI VE

Honor thy father and thy mother,
that thou mayest be long lived upon the land
which the Lord thy God will give thee.

The Fifth Commandment marks the transition from our relationship with God to a concentration on social relationships. One of the great purposes of parents is to raise their children to be men and women of God. This was God's intention from the beginning. Parents are the first ones we bond with and have a relationship with.

Good parents are our first and lifelong teachers, having our interest and well-being above their own. As children, parents are the most important people in our lives. They protect us, teach us, guide us and comfort us. They offer balance in child rearing by providing their unique perspective on life issues. And though we may not think of them in this way, they are our truest friends.

This commandment is not restricted to fathers and mothers, however. It concerns the flow of human relationships. To honor thy father and thy mother blueprints God's intended model for every relationship we will have, whether it be friend, family, business associate, neighbor, or spouse. It is the foundation for any decent society. It also acknowledges a chain of command and a show of respect for authority to which God is the author. When we honor our parents we offer our respect and obedience giving them a place of importance. We also honor God through our obedience to Him.

The spirit of this imperative views all behavior as either honorable, or dishonorable and establishes a pattern of behavior that acknowledges all human beings equally as God's work. If the attempt is made to honor and respect parents, that behavior will carry over to others. There are many ways to keep this commandment, however, by continually striving to live a righteous lifestyle avoids bringing shame and dishonor not only to parents, but to friends, social and work groups, family and ourselves.

SIX

Thou shalt not kill.

In reading the scriptures it becomes evident that this commandment is actually referring to the crime of murder, the legal definition of which has changed over time. Murder by definition today is; the unlawful killing of another human being without justification, or excuse. In the United States, murder comes in four varieties: intentional killing; killing resulting from intent to do bodily harm; killing resulting from jealousy, or extreme recklessness; and killing committed by an accomplice during the attempt, flight from, or commission of certain felonies.

There are many circumstances in which people kill other people. When God said Thou shalt not kill, He was telling the Hebrews not to willfully do anything that would take the life of another human being through murder. Thou shalt not kill is a behavioral instruction regarding how we should treat one another. God also stated; *He that striketh a man with a will to kill him, shall be put to death.* Ex. 21 vs. 12, further illustrating the point that no person has the right to murder another human being. This includes abortion. Although the word 'abortion' is not found in scripture, reading of the scriptures clearly indicates it is wrong. Life has a beginning and an end, and the beginning of our life starts at conception, not at birth. It is undeniable. God tells us he knows us before birth, even before conception.

Behold the inheritance of the Lord are children: the reward, the fruit of the womb.
Psalm 126 vs. 3.

I call heaven and earth to witness this day, that I have set before you life and death, blessing and cursing. Choose therefore life, that both thou and thy seed may live.
Deut. 30 vs. 19.

And the word of the Lord came to me, saying: Before I formed thee in the bowels of thy mother, I knew thee: and before thou camest forth out of the womb, I sanctified thee.
Jer. 1 vs. 4 – 5.

Killing, however, is not always murder and God provided justification for this. As an example;

If a thief be found breaking open a house or undermining it, and be wounded so as to die: he that slew him shall not be guilty of blood. Ex. 22 vs. 2.

Scripture provides examples of when killing is justified, as in cases involving the protection of life and property, defense of self, or defense of others, including killing as punishment for certain crime, known today as a capital offense, which is a form of self-defense of society. Even Jesus' disciples carried swords. So too, can war often be a matter of self-defense. Killing is never justified, however, to forward personal, political, ideological, or religious causes.

SEVEN
Thou shalt not commit adultery.

Adultery generally refers to sexual acts between a married person and someone who is not that person's spouse. And even though only one party might be married, the other is equally guilty of the sin. Though maybe not correct in the strictest technical sense, the term serves as a signpost that denotes all sex outside of marriage as wrong. For most of history adultery has been viewed as a crime often punishable by death, which included stoning. In England, having sexual relations with a sovereign's spouse, or even an heir to the throne is considered treason.

Regardless of cultural bias, application of law, or technical ambiguity, make no mistake, when God issued this command He meant its application to both men and women. And though it appears such, this commandment was not meant to be limited to the singularity of marriage.

In Moses time this commandment indirectly addressed certain pagan gods and rituals such as the worship of the goddess Ashteroth, or Astarte in which unmarried sexual activity played a significant role. It is as much a concern over sexual morality, as it is chastity, for sexual immorality (sex outside the sanctity of marriage) is frequently addressed in scripture where warnings abound. Whether it be movies, books, pictures, magazines, conversation, internet, or any other like areas, anything that contaminates one's thoughts, or strives with the flesh in terms of sex is subject to this command.

Adultery is not a victimless crime, between God and sinner alone. It has far reaching effects beginning with the aggrieved spouse followed by children, family, friends and work. Severe mental, physical, emotional and financial strains can be borne by all whom this sin touches. Adultery has three components. First, a lie is told. Deception must take place prior to the act. Those to whom the deception occurs must be lied to, to avoid getting caught. Second is the act which is referred to in contemporary slang as "cheating". The act itself is the culmination of the sin from which the third component emerges, stealing, which includes theft of security, peace, love and trust. The French Encyclopedia of Diderot & d'Alembert, Vol. 1 (1751) stated;

"adultery is, after homicide, the most punishable of all crimes, because it is the most cruel of all thefts, and an outrage capable of inciting murders and the most deplorable excesses." Hence the axiom; When you lie, you cheat. When you cheat, you steal. Adultery is a violation of commitment and the ultimate betrayal of all human relationships. Disregarding this commandment is an abandonment of morality in justification of satisfying the flesh.

EIGHT
Thou shalt not steal.

Prior to Exodus the time of man transpired as a period of survival of the strongest, whoever was most brutal, most powerful and often without regard for others. People had ideas about certain behaviors, but generally lacked any governance, or force of will beyond individual, or group ability. There was never a time when anyone fancied having their possessions taken from them, but there was little they could do without a code, or rule of law governing behavior that everyone recognized and was subject to. Force of power, usually found in a king, decided what behavior was acceptable, and how that behavior would be imposed, and it varied from king to king. Other than that, losing, or keeping one's possessions was often a matter of strength. Moses appeared at a point when God wanted to bring order into the world through His chosen people. The Commandments are the foundation of that order generating not only a code of law, but also a code of ethics and morality.

Stealing has several meanings in contemporary language. It could mean a great bargain, "this was a steal", or as a sports term, he stole home plate, or to be secretive, she stole away in the night, none of which are wrong in and of themselves. Stealing described in this commandment refers to criminal behavior, or theft, the taking of something belonging to someone else without the right, or permission to do so. This is a fairly straight forward mandate that very often accompanies lying and cheating. Yet the degree and the type of theft (corporate vs. personal) can diminish, or enhance the crime in the eyes of the law and the person doing the taking. But whether a cherry is sampled at the grocery store, small items from the workplace are consumed, taken, or offered to others, something unrelated is included in an insurance claim, hours not worked are padded to a timesheet, if done without right, or permission, it is the same as grand theft auto, or robbing a bank. Stealing is stealing regardless of degree.

Illegal gain, as with bribery, insider trading, or falsifying a tax return is also a form of stealing. More often than not, ethics violations involve stealing. And theft is not the mere separation of property from one entity to another. It is often an egregious invasion of privacy that deposits overwhelming confusion, fear, insecurity, anger and personal violation unmatched by most other crimes. The bottom line is that if a person takes, acquires, or transfers something which does not belong to them and is without right, regardless of degree, legality, or lack thereof, it is stealing in the eyes of God and a violation of His Commandment.

NINE

Thou shalt not bear false witness against thy neighbor.

To bear false witness is generally understood to mean making fictitious statements about a person, or giving untrue testimony in court, as when Jesus was arrested and falsely accused by the chief priests so they could put him to death. To avoid this is the clear intent of this Commandment. Yet, there is a larger standard implied here, which is, to avoid telling a lie. Another way to state this is tell the truth. Lying has potent social significance in that it is viewed as a flaw upon one's character. It is considered a crime when done under oath (perjury). Perjury is considered a serious offense in and of itself, regardless of the magnitude of the underlying case, or issue because it can undermine the justice system. It also destroys an individual's credibility and reputation, possessing the potential for adverse effects to other people and organizations. It can be argued that there may be instances when lying is morally permissible, but in normal everyday life honesty used with common sense is the best policy. That being said, it is hard to imagine an occasion when bearing false witness against a neighbor to do him harm is ever morally correct.

TEN

Thou shalt not covet thy neighbor's house:
neither shalt thou desire his wife, nor his servant, nor his handmaid,
nor his ox, nor his ass, nor any thing that is his.

Ancient Israel was patriarchal in structure dominated by the husband which is why the language sometimes is culturally specific to men. But as is repeatedly observed in scripture, God's laws, precepts and commands are not meant to be gender exclusive. To covet, in the present context, means to desire wrongfully. Aimed at the conscience, the mind and the heart, coveting enmeshes thoughts and feelings. This is a broad stroked imperative that covers lust and the improper desire of property, thoughts and feelings about which can lead to other types of crime such as lying, theft, adultery and murder.

The first known use of his word occurred in the fourteenth century. It is currently used to translate the Hebrew meaning of sinful desire in contrast to a sinful act. This solicits the question "Can thoughts be sinful?" Jesus elucidates the following;

You have heard that it was said to them of old: Thou shalt not commit adultery. But I say to you, that whosoever shall look on a woman to lust after her, hath already committed adultery with her in his heart. Matt 5 vs. 27 – 28.

Thoughts and feelings of desire are natural to people, and we are all occasionally tempted by them. They become sinful when we give in to them and allow them to progress beyond the point of temptation. We should flee from sinful thoughts, not entertain, or consider them.

But each person is tempted when they are dragged away by their own evil desire and enticed. Then, after desire has conceived, it gives birth to sin; and sin, when it is full-grown, gives birth to death. James 1 vs. 14 – 15. NIV.

This analysis is presented with the sincere belief and faith that the biblical account of the Ten Commandments is not myth, it is real history. They apply today as much as they did in Moses' time. The language of the Book of Exodus compellingly suggests it was God's intent that His law be perpetual. Jesus Himself spoke to this in the Sermon on the Mount when he said;

Do not think that I am come to destroy the law, or the prophets. I am not come to destroy, but to fulfill. For amen I say unto you, till heaven and earth pass, one jot, or one tittle shall not pass of the law, till all be fulfilled. He therefore that shall break one of these least commandments, and shall so teach men, shall be called the least in the kingdom of heaven. But he that shall do and teach, he shall be called great in the kingdom of heaven. Matt 5 vs. 17-19.

THE TEN COMMANDMENTS

Exodus Chap. 20 vs. 1–17

And the Lord spoke all these words:

ONE   I am the Lord thy God, who brought thee out of the land of Egypt, out of the house of bondage. Thou shalt not have strange gods before me.

TWO   Thou shalt not make to thyself a graven thing, nor the likeness of anything that is in heaven above, or in the earth beneath, nor of those things that are in the waters under the earth. Thou shalt not adore them, nor serve them: I am the Lord thy God, mighty, jealous, visiting the iniquity of the fathers upon the children, unto the third and fourth generation of them that hate me: And shewing mercy unto thousands to them that love me, and keep my commandments.

THREE   Thou shalt not take the name of the Lord thy God in vain: for the Lord will not hold him guiltless that shall take the name of the Lord his God in vain.

FOUR   Remember that thou keep holy the sabbath day. Six days shalt thou labor, and shalt do all thy works. But on the seventh day is the sabbath of the Lord thy God: thou shalt do no work on it, thou nor thy son, nor thy daughter, nor thy manservant, nor thy maidservant, nor thy beast, nor the stranger that is within thy gates. For in six days the Lord made heaven and earth, and the sea, and all things that are in them, and rested on the seventh day: therefore the Lord blessed the seventh day, and sanctified it.

FIVE   Honor thy father and thy mother, that thou mayest be long lived upon the land which the Lord thy God will give thee.

SIX   Thou shalt not kill.

SEVEN   Thou shalt not commit adultery.

EIGHT   Thou shalt not steal.

NINE   Thou shalt not bear false witness against thy neighbor.

TEN   Thou shalt not covet thy neighbor's house: neither shalt thou desire his wife, nor his servant, nor his handmaid, nor his ox, nor his ass, nor any thing that is his.

URL References

(1) http://www.todayifoundout.com Davin Hiskey

(2) http://www.jewfaq.org/whoisjew.htm

(3) http://en.wikipedia.org/wiki/Hebrews

(4) http://www.jewfaq.org/whoisjew.htm

(5) http://en.wikipedia.org/wiki/Bithiah

(6) http://en.wikipedia.org/wiki/Amenhotep_I

(7) http://en.wikipedia.org/wiki/Thutmose_II

(8) http://en.wikipedia.org/wiki/Mount_Sinai

(9) http://www.geographia.com/egypt/sinai/mtsinai.htm

(10) http://en.wikipedia.org/wiki/Rephidim

(11) http://www.bible.ca/archeology/bible-archeology-exodus-date-1440bc.htm

(12) http://www.drbo.org/

(13) http://www.gotquestions.org/golden-calf.html

(14) http://en.wikipedia.org/wiki/Moses/Michelangelo

www.ingramcontent.com/pod-product-compliance
Lightning Source LLC
Chambersburg PA
CBHW060550030426
42337CB00021B/4517